presentation

Brief Lessons and Inspiring Stories

A book to inspire and celebrate
your achievements.

By Jim Williamson

Edited by Dan Zadra
Designed by Kobi Yamada and Steve Potter
Compendium Inc.

DEDICATION

This book is dedicated to the mentors who guided me; the sales managers who challenged me; the clients who trusted me; the students who followed me; the colleagues who teamed with me; the partners who dreamed with me; and to my wife, Maxine, who believed in me.

ACKNOWLEDGEMENTS

The author and editors sincerely appreciate the following people who contributed invaluable assistance, spirit or content to Lessons Learned: John Becvar, Delores Bergstrom, Dick Beselin, Ron Butler, Tom Black, Steve Cheney, Debbie Cottrell, Ron Crawford, Don Daniels, Curt Dickerson, Cris Dippel, Don Dougherty, Ron Fox, David Haines, Elaine Harwell, Denny Holm, Kelly Holm, Cheryl Hungate, Dick Iversen, Gary Jacobson, Eric Jonson, Harry Mandros, Mark Matteson, Bob Moawad, John Moeller, Anna Nerbovig, Pat O'Day, Vince Pfaff, Dennis Schmahl, Janet Scroggs, Jack Sparacio, Dave Sund, Larry Sund, Ron Tarrant, Greg Tiemann, Lee Tillman, Don Williamson, and Dan Zadra.

WITH SPECIAL THANKS TO

Suzanne Hoonan, President, Advantage Learning, without whose creativity and guidance this book would still be merely a good idea.

CREDITS

Edited by Dan Zadra
Designed by Kobi Yamada and Steve Potter

TABLE OF CONTENTS

INTRODUCTION

*If I went back to school, I would focus on
two areas—communicating and presenting.
Mastering these opens so many doors.*

—*Former President Gerald Ford*

I often hear CEOs describe certain people in their company as "natural-born salespeople." My personal belief is that virtually *everyone* is a born salesperson. By the time we're in school, we are selling our friends on accepting us, selling our teachers on giving us good grades, and selling our parents on letting us stay out late on Friday night. Without any formal training, the typical teenager has already acquired a full complement of natural sales skills, including timing, persuasion, handling objections, negotiation and persistence. Some teenagers hone these skills and go on to become corporate or community leaders. Former President Bill Clinton was frequently described as a "salesman" by his detractors, as if that was supposed to be a character flaw. And yet a *Time Magazine* feature story on the top fifty leaders of the 20th Century suggests that the common denominator of all influential leaders is "a gift for presenting and selling their ideas."

You have this gift, too. You were born with it, and you have used it successfully all your life without really thinking about it. In the following pages you will discover some simple, proven reminders for converting this natural talent to a conscious and professional skill.

Everything you are about to read will be amplified if you sincerely believe in your product or service. When I truly believe that what I am representing is good for my customer, then I have put myself in the right frame of mind for presenting and selling my ideas. I never feel like I am imposing, or pushing or pressuring; I feel instead like I am doing him or her a favor or a service. One of the essays in this book encourages you to think of a good presentation as a "present" that you bring to your customer. That, in my mind, is the perfect metaphor for today's sales and service professional.

—Jim Williamson

COMPASS POINTS

If you don't know where you're going,
you might wind up someplace else.

—*Yogi Berra*

To ensure that you get the greatest possible value from this book, please take a few quiet minutes to complete the following reflective thinking exercise. A similar exercise is included at the end of the book.

1. My greatest strength in preparing and making presentations is:

_____

_____

2. One presentation situation I'd like to handle better:

_____

_____

3. The person whose presentation ability I most admire:

_____

4. The one quality (or qualities) I most admire about him or her:

_____

_____

5. If I get nothing else from this book, I'm going to keep an open mind and look for ways to improve the following:

_____

_____

A BOOK TO
INSPIRE AND CELEBRATE
YOUR ACHIEVEMENTS

COME TOGETHER

The words "information" and "communication"
are often used interchangeably, but they signify
quite different things. Information is giving out;
communication is getting through.

—*Sydney J. Harris*

The best presenters are usually the best communicators.
That may sound obvious, but there's more to it than you
might imagine.

What exactly is good communication? Ohio State University
researchers asked several hundred people to answer that
question. When all was said and done, the most common
denominator seemed to be the idea that good communication
must be "two way." And yet far too many sales presentations
are basically "one way" affairs.

Wait, there's more. Look up "communication" in the dictionary
and you will discover that it is actually derived from the same
ancient Latin root word as "communion"—which literally means
to "come together." People coming together for a two-way
exchange of ideas—that, to me, is a great guideline for
planning and preparing a blue-ribbon sales presentation.
But you seldom see it put into practice.

Far too many sales presentations are basically one-sided efforts to relay a lot of wonderful information to the other side. They may be loaded with valuable facts, figures, graphs and charts. But I have learned that there's a big difference between information and communication. As John Naisbitt reminded us, "People today are drowning in information, but starving for meaning."

The next time you plan a presentation, try using 25% of your time to convey the information, 25% to explore the potential meaning and significance of the information for your audience, and dedicate the remaining 50% of your time to help you and your audience come together in a free-wheeling two-way exchange of ideas. That exchange is where your presentation has the best and highest opportunity of moving naturally to an action step.

LESSONS LEARNED

- *Information is not necessarily communication.*
- *The best communication is "two-way."*
- *Ask questions; involve your audience; invite interaction.*

HEAD AND HEART

People do not live by pie charts, bar graphs or 300-page statistical reports alone. People live, reason and are moved by emotion, symbols and stories.

—*Tom Peters*

Logic and emotion are the Yin and Yang of every good presentation. Generally speaking, you need both—and common sense dictates how much of each.

In our sales seminars we advise our participants to give each of their presentations the "Baby Bear" test. If you remember your fairy tales, Papa Bear's bed was too hard...Mamma Bear's bed was too soft...but Baby Bear's bed was "just right."

Well, what we try to impress upon salespeople is that some presentations are too logical, and some are too emotional. Some are all heart, and some are all head. Some are too dry and boring, and some are too mushy and fluffy. Some are too weighted toward features and data, and some are too weighted toward benefits and romance. What you really want to do is balance them out so that the final presentation is "just right."

Of course, some say that you shouldn't weave emotional appeal into a presentation to a "left-brained" techno-organization such as Boeing or Microsoft. I disagree. Sure, Boeing engineers may need and appreciate left-brained data more than most—but don't ever think that they don't have big hearts, or that they aren't just as passionate about their work and their dreams.

Here's a good rule of thumb for evaluating whether your presentation or speech will move people to action: In general, people tend to trust and to follow those leaders who have their eyes on a star, but their feet on the ground. For most of humanity, that well-balanced combination of qualities feels "just right."

LESSONS LEARNED

- *Think, "Eyes on the stars, but feet on the ground."*
- *Present features _and_ benefits.*
- *Integrate logic _and_ emotion.*
- *Balance head _and_ heart.*

DREAM BUILDING

If you can dream it, you can do it.

—Walt Disney

Here's a provocative insight from Lloyd Allard: "Often, our customers are beaten down and discouraged. They have had to compromise because of the realities of life. When you prepare your sales presentations, try to rekindle the dreams that sparked your customers' initial desires. Incorporate your product or service into those dreams. Show them how, with your help, their dreams will come true."

Examples: I know of a computer software rep who sold a system-wide installation to a national HMO by uncovering a long-held dream of the Human Resources Director. The dream was to improve quality work life by providing her employees with an internal communication network that would allow them to help each other balance their workloads and their lives. My friend's software wasn't originally designed to do that, but he simply adapted it to the dream.

I know an international freight handler who stopped to help a small British publisher fulfill her dream of distributing her books in the United States. By connecting her with the right U.S. distributor, he landed all subsequent shipping contracts with her thanks.

And yes, I even know a plumbing supply representative who convinced a young Seattle facilities manager that he could save his job during a company-wide layoff. Together, they presented a bold plan to switch out the company's plumbing and hydraulics, thereby slashing manufacturing costs in the plant by nearly twenty percent.

How can *you* and *your* products be presented to help people rediscover and rekindle their dreams?

LESSONS LEARNED

- *Every customer has dreams and aspirations.*
- *Start with their dream and work backwards to your product.*
- *Dreams move people to action.*

ASSUMPTIONS

*The height of your accomplishment will
usually equal the depth of your preparation.*

—*Andrew Scoville*

Years ago I worked for Prentice-Hall. It was a beehive of activity and opportunity, constantly buzzing with new book ideas, co-marketing possibilities and presentations.

In that kind of accelerated environment, a salesperson doesn't always have the luxury of gathering a thorough scouting report on the next prospective client. But that is one discipline that is sure to come back and bite you if you let it slide. To emphasize the point, Ray Cody, our National Sales Manager, openly related the following sales blunder to every new recruit:

One year Ray had just received in-depth training on a new music series. There was a huge school curriculum adoption opportunity in the fall, and Ray got on the calendar to present our series. He was fully prepared and gave what he thought was an outstanding presentation—all to the blank stares of every school administrator in the audience.

Finally, the curriculum director himself mercifully interrupted. "Ray, it sounds like Prentice-Hall has a very fine elementary music series, but we are adopting mathematics this year. You're more than welcome to come back in two years when we are evaluating music education."

Yes, Ray was thoroughly embarrassed, but he always ended his story by saying that he never made another presentation again without first finding time to qualify the audience and the situation in advance.

LESSONS LEARNED:

- *Scouting reports win games.*
- *Thoroughly qualify every audience in advance.*
- *Tailor your presentation to their needs, not yours.*

METAPHORS

Selling is like cooking. Sometimes you
follow the recipe, and sometimes you're creative.

—*Roger von Oech*

Most salespeople have been using sports metaphors for years.
We team up, tee off, have kickoff meetings, hit home runs, give
knockout performances, and bring home the gold.

But well-chosen metaphors can also be spectacular presentation tools. If you have a complex product or program,
a metaphor can make it simple.

Metaphors are especially helpful for explaining ideas to people
outside your specialty. For example, when the Dolby Stereo
sound system was first introduced, the marketers used a
laundry metaphor to make the technology more understand-
able and user-friendly to the public: "Think of Dolby as an
incredibly efficient sonic laundry. It washes dirt (or noise) out
of the signal, leaving the sound that reaches your ears clean
and pure."

A friend of mine markets "Internal Communication Programs for Corporate America." That sounds way too complex and boring for most people, so my friend has adopted a "fire" metaphor to explain it. His sales promise sounds like this: "If you are a CEO, our communication process will help you build one central fire inside your organization. In the middle of the fire is your company Vision and Mission. Once lit, that fire will warm the hearts and minds of your employees, and it will act as a beacon to attract more customers to your products and services."

It's easy, fun and effective to weave metaphors into your presentations. Today, answer the following question in five or ten colorful ways: *Our product or service is like a...*

LESSONS LEARNED

- *Audiences love a good, strong metaphor.*
- *Metaphors are "word pictures."*
- *Use them to inspire, educate and motivate.*

PIZZA OR HEAT?

Now and then, it's a good idea to stop
and analyze what you're actually selling.

—Tom Peters

If you have a new or unusual product to present, you know how difficult it can be to educate the public. When the first microwave ovens were introduced, the product should have blown right off the shelves. Instead, you could hear the laughter from coast-to-coast. Literally thousands of live presentations were conducted throughout the country to prove that a potato could be cooked in 10 minutes, and water could be boiled in seconds. But the wrong thing was being presented!

Finally the manufacturers figured out that the public was really saying, "I get it, but I don't trust it. It can't be a good idea to cook my dinner with a nuclear blast." From that point on, the manufacturers focused on marketing and presenting "safety" instead of the oven itself.

It can be just as tricky to market a familiar product that has been around for decades. I once attended a franchise opportunity meeting conducted by Domino's Pizza—but there was actually very little mention of pizza that day. Here's the wonderful lesson I learned:

Like all pizza, Domino's pizza has gooey cheese and toppings. It looks, tastes and costs about the same as other delivered pizzas, but Domino's dominates. Why? Because Domino's pizza arrives "piping hot" at your door in about 60 minutes in a special insulated container. Let's face it, pizza is pizza, and Domino's sells pizza—but what they're *really* marketing are location, convenience, speed and heat.

Today, ask yourself, "What am I *really* marketing and selling? All other things being equal, which features or benefits could I emphasize in my presentations in order to dominate my marketplace?

LESSONS LEARNED:

- *Marketing is trying to have what people want.*
- *Sales is trying to get people to want what you have.*
- *World's most important question: "What am I really marketing, selling and presenting?"*

RELATIVITY

A problem or opportunity is always relative.
Your toothache feels terrific to the dentist.
—*Ramona Arnett*

Mark McCormack, the CEO of International Marketing Group, wrote a street-smart book entitled, *What They Don't Teach You At Harvard Business School.* Here's one of his tips for preparing sensible, hard-hitting presentations: "A salesperson must practice a kind of theory of relativity. He or she must constantly ask, 'Compared to what?'"

Translation: When preparing a sales proposal, start with the premise that every single product or service, including *yours*, costs too much—until you compare it to something else. If you're selling homes, every house is outrageously overpriced, until you compare it to the price of a similar house...or to its resale value...or to what someone else is ready to offer...or to what the customer deserves, etc.

The same principle applies if you are offering a consulting service. Paying $1,000 to attend a one-day sales workshop may seem exorbitant, but not when compared to the results achieved. Demonstrate that the typical graduate of your course enjoys a 20 percent increase in sales, and that $1,000 suddenly becomes a bargain compared to the value received.

Even my plumber practices the theory of relativity. His estimate of $90 per hour to repair my curtain drain initially gave me sticker shock...until he patiently explained what my foundation would look like if he *didn't* repair it.

Today, nearly everything is perceived as expensive—because it is! It's your job to present and position your products and services in a meaningful frame of reference that will help your customers quickly perceive the comparative *value* as well as the price.

LESSONS LEARNED

- *Price is always relative.*
- *All products should be evaluated in a bigger frame of reference.*
- *If you don't create the frame of reference, your customer will.*

BE SPECIFIC

If you can't measure it,
you can't manage or market it.
—*Jim Scase*

A band of New York book publishers was invited to tour the plant of a large paper mill that supplied many New York publishers with paper. The sales manager hosted a dozen publishers who accepted the invitation. The food was excellent, the wine flowed freely, and when the sales manager rose to make his presentation, he was applauded warmly by both the guests and his sales force.

"Ladies and gentlemen," he said with a sentimental catch in his voice, "just fifteen years ago today our mill received its very first paper order from a New York book publisher."

At that moment a salesman in the rear of the room piped up, "And when are you going to fulfill it?"

The story illustrates a huge, but often unspoken concern of your prospects. If you're working on a capabilities proposal for your company, nothing speaks louder on your behalf than specifics. If there's a question about when you expect to deliver, lay it right out there in black and white—and the more specific, the better.

"Next day delivery" was too vague for Federal Express customers, so FedEx specified 10:30 a.m.

"Quick service" was too vague for bank customers, so Bank of America created its "5-minute teller" guarantee.

The list goes on. Disney theme parks are swept clean "every 30 minutes." EMPAQ employees answer every phone call "within three rings," and respond to every customer letter "within 24 hours."

The next time you make a presentation, try to weave in some clear, specific and compelling numbers with your promise.

LESSONS LEARNED

- *Quantify your promises.*
- *Be specific.*
- *Live up to them.*

UNDER-PROMISE
AND OVER-DELIVER

A promise made must be a promise kept.
—*Mass Mutual Ad*

Don Daniels is a co-founder of Shurgard Storage Centers, and the founder of On-Guard Mini-Storage. Don has made more Limited Partnership investment presentations than anyone I know. Those who invest with Don—and there's quite a list— usually invest more than once. For this book I asked Don to share his number one success principle in 200 words or less. He did it in three: *Under-promise and Over-deliver.*

If salespeople follow human nature—and they usually do—the natural tendency in any presentation will be to paint the rosiest picture possible. But even if that picture is credible, Don will always tone it down a notch or two.

"If I show a potential investor a 7-year forecast on a typical mini-storage investment," Don explains, "I always under-estimate what the investment yields are likely to be. If I expect an annual cash return of 15% to the Limited Partners, my presentation might show 10% ('under-promise'). If I expect the future sale of the project to result in a 200% return, my presentation might show 150% (again, 'under-promise').

"Then, when the actual financial results are achieved, the investor experiences an overall investment return that exceeds his expectations ('over-deliver'). Result: This makes a hero of the General Partner, and a happier investor who is then ready to make another mini-storage investment."

The next time you make a presentation, resist the temptation to appear like a hero today, and think instead about tomorrow. By setting the bar at a more reasonable height, you'll build a long-term reputation for not just meeting, but exceeding, your implied promise to your customer.

LESSONS LEARNED

- *Resist the temptation to over-promise.*
- *If you surprise your customer, surprise to the upside.*
- *Make it a habit to exceed customer expectations.*

GOOD NEWS/BAD NEWS

People don't resist their own ideas.
—*Jan Bedore*

A good friend creates custom direct mail programs, and he has developed a unique strategy for handling objections: Identify the most likely reason why others might oppose your concept, and then bring it up *before* you detail the program to them. If, for example, he anticipates that "price-per-unit" will be today's top objection, the front end of his presentation might sound like this:

"I promised to create a direct mail concept that would out-pull any mailer your company has tried. The good news is that I'm about to show you that program. The bad news is that the cost per mailer is more than I anticipated.

"Now, I've been thinking about the problem and I've come up with a possible solution—but I need your help. If we can put our heads together and find a good reason to produce this mailer in larger quantities, the economies of a higher print run will easily drive the cost per mailer down. So, as I detail the concept over the next few minutes, please be thinking about additional applications—creative ways to get your quantities up, and drive your cost per unit down."

By identifying the objection and solution up-front—and openly asking for help—he has changed the chemistry of the presentation and focused the collective imagination of the group on "finding a way." Instead of focusing on why they *can't* embrace his program, they immediately set to work on how they *can.*

Feeding artificial problems to your customers is a ploy. But inviting them to collaborate with you on removing a legitimate obstacle to a mutually desired solution is brilliant.

LESSONS LEARNED

- *Take your client on a crusade.*
- *Identify the dragon.*
- *Slay the dragon together.*

GIFTS

The old "foot in the door" school of selling
has gone the way of the dinosaur.
Sales today is all about giving, not taking.

—*Ian Fielder*

Active Markets Inc. upgraded their accounting system, eliminating a bookkeeping position in the process. June, the bookkeeper, loved Active Markets and wanted to stay on.

June was thrilled when the company offered her a telemarketing position. Her new role was to cold-call new accounts. Over the first few days June practiced her presentation and impressed the sales manager with her clear command of the company's capabilities. When it came time to make calls, however, she couldn't bring herself to dial the numbers.

She explained her reluctance to her manager. "I love this company," she stammered, "but I can't stand people who call out of the blue to sell you stuff you don't even need. I can't be one of those."

Her manager's comforting response re-centered June and cleared the way for a successful career in sales: "We don't want you to be one of those, either," he said. "Our services are unique in the industry, and we offer them only to people who can actually benefit. The truth is, nearly everyone on that list would probably give you a hug if they truly understood what Active Markets can do for them. The problem is that no one has ever told them about us—and that's the gift you are bringing to them."

A good reminder for all of us: As you dial that phone, think of your presentation as a "present" that you are delivering with all good intention. Your motive is not to trick, sell, badger or win—your motive is to give a gift. Present that gift clearly, confidently and thoughtfully—as only you can do.

LESSONS LEARNED

- *Think of your presentation as a "present."*
- *Act only with good motives and high intention.*
- *Sales is about giving, not taking.*

FEARLESS

*It is paradoxical, but profoundly true,
that the best way to relieve our own fear
and anxiety is by turning our focus outward
and doing something good for others.*

—John Holmes

One day my company had a big presentation scheduled for a group of bankers. Our rep was a terrific speaker, and the bankers were all anxious to hear him. Unfortunately, the rep came down with the flu that morning. His only option was to call upon our first-year rookie consultant to make the presentation in his place.

On the drive to the event site, the rookie had thirty minutes to come to terms with the assignment and to somehow prepare his presentation. He was terrified, and he called to tell me so: "Jim, I'm only 23, these bankers will take one look at me and think it's a waste of time."

The only thing that came to my mind turned out to be the right advice: "You know the material as well as anyone. Do not apologize for who you are. Quit thinking about yourself, and focus instead on those bankers. Your only job is to do the best job you can for them. Just know in your heart that, whatever happens, your motives are good, and you are making this presentation for all the right reasons. The rest will take care of itself."

Later that day he called me again. "What happened?" I asked. "The presentation went fantastic and I was invited back," he said proudly.

My experience is that most audiences are very forgiving. They will quickly rally to support a presenter who may not be one hundred percent prepared or polished...as long as he or she is open, honest, caring and one hundred percent focused on the audience rather than themselves.

LESSONS LEARNED

- *Average presenters focus on themselves.*
- *Good presenters focus on their material.*
- *Great presenters focus on their audience.*
- *Reach out to others and they will reach back to you.*

31

BUTTERFLIES

*Ultimately we know that the other side
of every fear is a freedom.*

—Marilyn Ferguson

The *Book of Lists* has a section on the Top 10 Fears. Number 4 on the list is death, and number 1 is public speaking. My friend, Jack Sparacio, interprets this to mean that most people attending a funeral would rather be the person in the coffin than the person giving the eulogy.

In our Presentation seminars someone always stands up and asks, "How can I overcome my fear of speaking?" My answer: "Don't try to overcome it; try to use it. A little fear is actually a good thing; it keeps you focused. It's the *absence* of fear that's dangerous."

For example, a well-known rock climber recently fell to his death here in Washington. Several days later a radio talk show discussed the tragedy. One caller who was a climber and a former fighter pilot said, "I knew the climber who died, and unfortunately I believe he had gotten too complacent, he literally knew no fear. One thing they taught us in fighter school is to always be just a little scared to stay sharp."

The same principle applies to public presentations. A little fear is your friend. Welcome it. Manage it. Use it. Like the old saying goes, "It's all right to have butterflies, just make sure they fly in formation."

Seven trusty reminders: 1. Know your subject. 2. Practice, practice, practice. 3. Rehearse in front of a mirror, then in front of someone. 4. Scan your audience; focus on a few friendly faces. 5. Smile and breathe. 6. Present as though you are speaking to one or two good friends. 7. Feel the fear and do it anyway.

LESSONS LEARNED

- *A little fear is good.*
- *It keeps you sharp.*
- *Welcome, manage and use it!*

QUESTIONS

I use the Columbo approach to questioning:
"Maybe you can help me understand something
that's unclear to me...? What is...?
Really? Tell me more..."

—David Haines, International Business Consultant

Enjoy this $30-million piece of advice from my good friend
David Haines, a prominent corporate accountant:

"A major manufacturer invited four companies, mine included,
to present to a committee consisting of six decision makers.
Each company was given two weeks to prepare their
presentation and could only communicate with one person—
the manufacturer's paralegal. When I asked who was going to
be making the final decision, the paralegal responded, "We all
are." When I asked for the criteria for winning the work, the
response was, "I can't say, but we're using a matrix system."
When I asked three times, "Tell me more, tell me more," the
paralegal responded, "Well, what I *can* say is we're using a
weighting system and you need to figure out which category
we assign more weight to: Price, Product, Customer Service,
Quality of Presentation, and Understanding Our Needs.

Armed with this scouting report I arrived at the conference room 90 minutes early to discover I was the first of the four finalists to present. In 60 minutes I managed to speak separately with five of the six committee members, asking key questions and clarifying each person's personal and professional stake in the outcome. During my introduction I asked if the committee would permit an interactive, two-way dialog, rather than a one-way conversation and presentation. All said, "Sure, but you only have 90 minutes to complete your presentation."

Some people believe "first in/first out." But I won this 30-million-dollar contract for my company by being the only person among the four finalists who took the time to ask Columbo-style questions in advance.

LESSONS LEARNED

- *He who has the most information wins.*
- *Ask naïve questions; keep asking.*
- *Persist, dig deeply, and prepare accordingly.*

COMPRESS IT

If you can't write your entire idea
on the back of your business card,
you don't have an idea.

—Don Belasco

We should all tip our hats to the person who first came up with the term, "elevator pitch." It's a great image, and a critical sales skill—the ability to compress the core essentials of your entire sales presentation into the brief time it takes to travel from one floor to another on an elevator.

How compressed can your presentation become, and still get the point across? Jay Conrad Levinson suggests that you practice encapsulating your key sales concept into a maximum of seven words. I've collected a few examples here to stir your creative juices.

Coca-Cola's turn-of-the-century two-word marketing plan: *"Bottle it."* Avis Rent-A-Car's brilliant three-word positioning statement: *"We try harder."* Sears Roebuck's 19th century catalog marketing breakthrough: *"Satisfaction guaranteed, or your money back."* Federal Express' astonishing seven-word logistical insight: *"Fly all packages to one central hub."*

Frank Perdue, who has sold millions and millions of chickens, cheated by using ten words instead of seven: *"It takes a tough man to make a tender chicken."*

None of these insights was easy to implement, but every one of them was easy to understand, and that's the point. Not a lot of words, but we all know exactly what they're selling.

LESSONS LEARNED

- *Compress the core essentials of your sales presentation.*
- *Encapsulate your "big idea" in a few words.*
- *Keep your message clear and simple.*

PLAIN TALK

What did you have for breakfast?
The upper part of a hog's hind leg with
two oval bodies encased in a shell laid
by a female bird—or ham and eggs?

—Harry Grey

Some of the best words are also the simplest. Take these words: "I have good news for you." Or these: "The budget was approved." Or these: "We're moving ahead with your project."

These simple elegant words trigger wonderful images and emotions in a salesperson's mind and heart. Why, then, do we insist on using complex jargon when presenting to our customers?

A story by Tom Peters illustrates how a good idea can still fail unless it is sold (communicated) simply and clearly: SAS Airlines named its discount program "Airfare F50" to signify 50% off—but Airfare F50 flopped. Later, SAS revived the program but renamed it the "Twenty Dollar Plan" which clearly described the actual fare. Switching from technical to plain talk caused the program to catch fire in the minds of consumers.

SAS Chairman, Jan Carlson, once remarked, "What people don't understand doesn't exist." I agree. A charter member of the Million Dollar Roundtable once told me, "Twenty percent of my customers are afraid to tell me that they don't know the difference between an insurance dividend and a premium. I don't talk baby talk to my customers, but I do ensure that they clearly understand what I'm selling."

Could it be that some of your customers simply don't get it? What technical jargon could you eliminate, clarify or enliven to help your sales and marketing presentations catch fire?

LESSONS LEARNED

- *Keep your message uncomplicated.*
- *Say what you mean; say only what you mean.*
- *Test your message; check for blind spots.*

PREPARATION

Six honest, faithful friends have I;
they are Who, What, When,
Where, How and Why?

—Anon

Don Lusk of Lusk and Associates related the following story regarding his making a formal sales presentation to a rather conservative group of CPA's. A large Manhattan accounting firm was preparing to develop the top 20 percent of their partners into becoming more effective "rainmakers." The screening committee had narrowed their search to three competing training and development organizations, one of which would be selected to customize a series of training seminars.

All three organizations, including Don's, were invited to New York to deliver a formal presentation to a committee of five. Each organization's representatives were allotted a maximum of one hour to present.

As part of Don's planning and preparation long before he flew to New York, he asked himself, "If I were a member of that committee, what criteria would be most important to me?"

Don then took a calculated risk. He built his entire presentation around five key criteria that he thought might be on their list. Not only that, he opened his presentation to the committee by relating to them what he had done.

The result? Don discovered that four out of five on his list were also on the committee's list. In short he said, " I had their attention, delivered one of my best presentations and was awarded the contract."

LESSONS LEARNED:

- *Analyze and know your audience.*
- *Brainstorm the main ideas you want to present in advance.*
- *Empathize. Ask yourself, "If I were in that audience, what would be most important to me?"*
- *Build your sales presentation around the audiences' criteria, not yours.*

THE BASICS

Public speaking, at its best,
is simple but not easy.

—Gil Atkinson

Matthew Perry, who catalogued speeches for three different U.S. Presidents, once remarked, "A well-written speech is a work of art, but a well-delivered speech is a work of heart." How true that is!

In our workshops, we use the following exercise to take some of the mystery and complexity out of public speaking. We call it "The Basics," and here's how it works:

Start by putting yourself in the shoes of the audience. There are three basic questions an audience will ask themselves about any speaker. These questions are asked sub-consciously and very quickly, right after you begin your presentation: 1. Do I like this speaker? 2. Do I understand this speaker? 3. Do I believe this speaker?

Now think of the last time you were in an audience and the speaker was in front of you. Ask yourself the three questions above in the past tense. What did that speaker do or not do to win me over? What conclusions did you reach? Now compare those conclusions with the following research:

Top 5 Characteristics of Successful Presenters: 1) Exude enthusiasm and passion for their message. 2) Manage the attention of the audience on the main message. 3) Inject some fun and humor into the presentation. 4) Connect with the audience personally and professionally. 5) Interact with the audience.

Those are the basics. Mastering the basics is fairly simple. Refining them is a work of heart that never ends.

LESSONS LEARNED

- *It all boils down to caring and preparing.*
- *Be passionate about your message.*
- *Care about your audience.*
- *Connect the two.*

MYTHS

Eight years ago my friend, Dick Iversen, of the Boeing Company received the following handout from a Harvard Ph.D. at an executive seminar. Dick has passed it on to many presenters, including a number of U.S. Senators and Congressmen:

Myth #1: "More is better."
Reality: "Less is more."

    1) Less data = more power. (3 main points)

    2) Visual aids (10 seconds = full understanding)

    3) Fewer words, but well-chosen (sound bites)

    4) Target audience small and well-profiled

    5) Concise message (Keep it simple superstars!)

Myth #2: "Audience hangs on my every word."
Reality: "Regaining attention is my job."

    1) 8 seconds (average adult attention span)

    2) 30 seconds (maximum adult attention span)

    3) Gain attention; regain it again and again.

Myth #3: "Hold hard copies to the end."
Reality: "Hard copies occupy wandering thoughts."

Typical audience is thinking about:

1) Erotic thoughts (22%)
2) Lunch (18%)
3) Never-never land (23%)
4) Religion (8%)
5) Your topic (17%)
6) Actively listening (12%)

We live in changing times. What worked well for yesterday's audience may not work in today's faster-paced environment.

LESSONS LEARNED

- *Be credible.*
- *Be flexible.*
- *Be clear.*
- *Clarity and persuasiveness come with specificity.*

CONNECT

Great presenters focus on making
emotional connections with their audience.

—Max Ernst

I remember a popular television commercial with a great
message for every professional presenter. A rock band comes
on stage, the applause is thunderous, the strobe lights are
flashing and the lead musician yells, "WE LOVE YOU DETROIT!"
Suddenly the audience goes silent and the camera scans a sea
of startled faces. Then one of the back-up musicians whispers,
"Dude, this isn't Detroit; we're in St. Paul." *Bam!* An immediate
disconnect with the audience.

Now let's recall a different dude—one of the all-time masters of
personal connection—the one and only Bob Hope. For more
than fifty years Hope was welcomed by people of all ages on
every continent, and he made personal friends with every U.S.
President, from Roosevelt to Clinton. His secret? Whether you
loved him or not, he had a way of showing that he knew and
cared about *you.*

If Hope went to Saigon to entertain the troops, he knew which K-rations tasted the worst. In Boise, he knew the inside scoop on this year's potato festival. In Louisiana, he knew Cajun jokes and even Cajun cuss-words.

How can you form a sincere personal connection with your audience or client? It's not so difficult. Do your research. Something personal, something wonderful, an interest or commitment unique to them—go and find it. Then acknowledge it in your presentation.

Has your client's company made a commitment to the ecology...or to pursuing the Baldridge Award for Quality... or to caring about the Special Olympics? Bring it up! Let them know that those are the kinds of things that you care about, too.

LESSONS LEARNED

- *Research your audience in advance.*
- *What makes them tick, proud, happy, sad, excited?*
- *Care, tailor and connect accordingly.*

KEY LINES

Put handles on your most important idea.
Make it easy for people to carry it away with them.
—*John Sculley*

Some of the most memorable thoughts are also the shortest. "God Bless America" is just three words, but three are all that's required. The Gettysburg Address has 271 words; the Ten Commandments have 297; the marriage vow just two.

My point? Whether you're writing a 20-minute speech or a 10-page proposal, here's one way to make your presentation stand out from all the rest: Take time to craft a single scintillating sentence that everyone will want to hold on to and remember!

You may not remember their entire presentations, but you remember these key lines:

Franklin Roosevelt after Pearl Harbor: *"Dec. 7, 1941—a day that will live in infamy."*

John F. Kennedy on his inauguration day: *"Ask not what your country can do for you."*

Martin Luther King at the Lincoln Memorial: *"I have a dream."*

Lee Iacocca on the day Chrysler repaid its loan from America: *"Chrysler borrows money the old fashioned way—we pay it back."*

Your key line doesn't have to be immortal, but it should leave people with a good reason to remember you and your distinguishing characteristic. A friend of mine in the pharmaceutical business was competing against the biggest names in the industry, and he knew that most of the people in his audience had barely even heard of his company. His key line: "Over the years we've quietly and uneventfully delivered nearly a billion individual doses of prescription medication. Does it bother us, then, when people say they've never heard our name? No, because in our business, if you're making mistakes, the whole world knows your name."

LESSONS LEARNED

- *What you say is important.*
- *What your audience remembers is more important.*
- *Leave them with one unforgettable idea.*

BACKUPS

Be prepared! It's better to have it and
not need it, than to need it and not have it.

—Elizabeth Ann Nolan

ARCO has invested millions in their long-term sponsorship of
the Olympic Games. One year Dan Zadra, my editor, was
invited to compete with several other creative people to design
a portion of ARCO's expansive sponsorship package.

On the appointed day, Dan flew into San Francisco with his
tightly choreographed 20-minute presentation tucked inside a
hefty presentation case. He took a cab to the big pyramid-
shaped building, rode the elevator to the top, and was
immediately hustled to an impressive conference room.
Several ARCO exec's sat stiffly around the table. There was
tension in the room; something was definitely wrong.

"Welcome to ARCO, Mr. Zadra" said the host, "we appreciate
your participation in our RFP. Unfortunately, most of our
committee will be flying out early afternoon for an unexpected
meeting. For this reason we are asking all designers to limit
their presentations to six minutes instead of 20."

Our story has a happy ending. Dan set his 20-minute version aside and pulled a pre-planned five-minute version from his portfolio. His backup presentation was crisp and complete, with adequate time to show four key visuals, ending with a clearly articulated summation. He was invited back for a second presentation and eventually won the contract.

Make it a rule with every presentation to have a condensed version at your fingertips. As they say, "Don't leave home without it." The same holds true for speaking engagements. If your remarks are scheduled for the end of a program, have two versions of your speech—one much shorter than the other. If the program runs long, go with the shorter one.

LESSONS LEARNED

- *Always have a condensed version of your speech or presentation available.*

- *Practice delivering both versions.*

- *Incorporate visuals; more will be remembered by what was seen versus heard.*

CLEAR THE FOG

To super-size your presentation,
down-size your sentences.
—*American Management Association*

You work hard to make your stand-up presentations clear, cogent and credible—but what about your *written* presentations? After you leave the room or the building, that written proposal becomes your on-site ambassador, quite possibly determining the fate of your ideas or project.

The Golden Rule for amplifying the power of a written presentation is supposed to be "keep it short," but I disagree. I have learned that clients often appreciate a longer proposal— one that covers all the bases and answers all their questions. And they will read every word if you simply follow the *real* Golden Rule, which is "keep it clear."

The *Fog Index* is a useful little tool I acquired from "The Great Book of Business Secrets." You can use it to measure how clearly your own proposals are written. Here's how it works:

Pick a 100-word section.

Count the number of sentences and divide 100 by that number. This gives you the average words per sentence.

Count the words with more than two syllables. Add this figure to the average words per sentence.

Multiply the total by 0.4 to get the Fog Index (which is the minimum school grade level a reader needs to comprehend it).

In general, the lower the index the better. A score of 11-12 is okay for most business letters or proposals. The Fog Index for my previous 100 words is 7.4.

LESSONS LEARNED

- *Go back and edit your written proposals.*
- *Eliminate big words or unnecessary jargon.*
- *"Keep it clear" is the Golden Rule.*

TOOLS

*Using Stone Age presentation technology
to sell 21st Century products or services
does not build credibility.*

—Jim Rouleau, Nova Corp.

I proudly proclaim that I'm a lifelong learner. One of my favorite mantras in our workshops is, "School is never out for the pro." And yet, for no good reason, I've been one of the last to embrace the evolution to high-tech computerized presentation techniques.

In the beginning, I rationalized my attachment to the "old ways" by claiming that my trusty flip charts and overlays were "high-touch." It sounds good. High-touch is always more personal and compelling than high-tech, right? Not any more.

A veteran sales pro recently lost six consecutive contracts to competitors using new computerized presentation aids—and for good reason. A little laptop can carry a mighty big, beautiful and powerful presentation. Equally important, it can instantaneously connect a salesperson in the field to critical data and inventory information that may have an immediate bearing on the outcome of today's presentation.

In the past, salespeople often needed hours or even days to respond to clients' questions. "I'll get those case histories and inventory numbers to you first thing tomorrow morning." That statement used to be a demonstration of responsiveness, but now it's almost an insult. Armed with a laptop, some or all of your competitors can instantly and graphically provide those answers to your busy clients with just a few keystrokes. Computers are God's gift to personalized service, too. I'm told that Ritz Carlton tracks personal preferences (favorite rooms, snacks, reading materials, etc.) for 500,000 frequent guests. Every major airline tracks special meals and mileage plans for thousands of passengers. A leading insurance agent in my city tracks the dreams and plans of several hundred families—all on his $1,500 laptop.

Resolve today that your clients deserve the best, clearest and fastest information or presentation you can provide. The tools are out there, now, so please investigate, use and enjoy them.

LESSONS LEARNED

- *School is never out for the pro.*
- *The world is advancing; advance with it.*
- *Stop right now and sharpen your saw.*

COMPASS POINTS

We can do more than work, we can grow.
—Suzanne Hoonan

1. The 5 most important ideas I gained from this book:

_____

_____

_____

2. Specific techniques, ideas, skills or strategies I will develop and put into practice:

_____

_____

_____

3. If I do nothing else but apply the value received from one lesson, that lesson is:

_____

_____

_____

**NINETY PERCENT
OF LEADERSHIP IS THE
ABILITY TO COMMUNICATE
SOMETHING PEOPLE WANT.**

—DIANE FEINSTEIN

ABOUT ADVANTAGE LEARNING SERVICES

ALS is a Seattle based training management and consulting firm formed to assist companies and their employees in achieving greater levels of performance and effectiveness.

Over the past 20 years ALS has developed and continues to offer in-depth seminars in the following areas:
• Leadership • Team Development • Attitude Development • Sales Management • Change Management • Sales • Service
• Presentation • Negotiation

ALS has a national account base, many of which participate in their certified train-the-trainer programs. The following is a partial list of our clients:

AT&T	Coca–Cola USA	Weyerhaeuser
Micron	Qwest	I.B.M.
Bank of America	Discover Card	Xerox
Microsoft	U.S. Bank	Lucent
Boeing	Hospital Corp. of	
Nike	America	

Other published products offered by Advantage Learning Services:

"Lessons Learned" Personal Library Series:
I. Sales. II. Service. III. Presentation. IV. Negotiation

Audio/CD/Video/DVD Programs:
• *Increasing Human Effectiveness* • *Team Development*
• *Assessments and Cultural Audits*

LOOKING FOR A KEYNOTE SPEAKER?

Would you like to make these books and other high interest topics come alive at your next sale or service meeting?

ALS provides a number of high interest Keynote Presentations in live multi-media format that will keep your audience's attention, assisting in your meeting's success. Four very popular keynote presentations at this time are:

- *Characteristics of High Performance Salespeople*
- *Gut-Level Leadership*
- *Managing Change in a Competitive Marketplace*
- *Maintaining Winning Attitudes In Turbulent Times*

To discuss availability, contact us at:

Advantage Learning Services
6947 Coal Creek Parkway, Suite 2600
Newcastle, WA 98059-3136

Phone: 425-747-4484
E-mail: advlerarn@worldnet.att.net

Visit us online today and experience our instant Culture Audit at www.advlearnsys.com

ABOUT THE AUTHOR

Photo Christine Scholz

Jim Williamson is co-founder and CEO of Advantage Learning Services, a private consulting and training organization based in Seattle, Washington.

Prior to founding ALS, Jim served as Sr. Vice-President of Sales & Marketing for Edge Learning Institute, currently an alliance business partner. He also served as District Sales Manager and, later, Director of Marketing for Prentice Hall's Educational Book Division in Englewood Cliffs, New Jersey. Earlier in his professional career he worked as a psychology teacher/guidance counselor at a high school, community college and Washington State prison.

Currently he specializes in the area of helping to develop High Performance Sales & Service Cultures within organizations. He has designed, written and published a number of customized sales and service programs which have been distributed to thousands of employees over the past 20 years.

Do you have a favorite story you'd like to submit? We would like to hear and consider your "lessons learned" for a future edition. Please submit to: advlearn@worldnet.att.net.